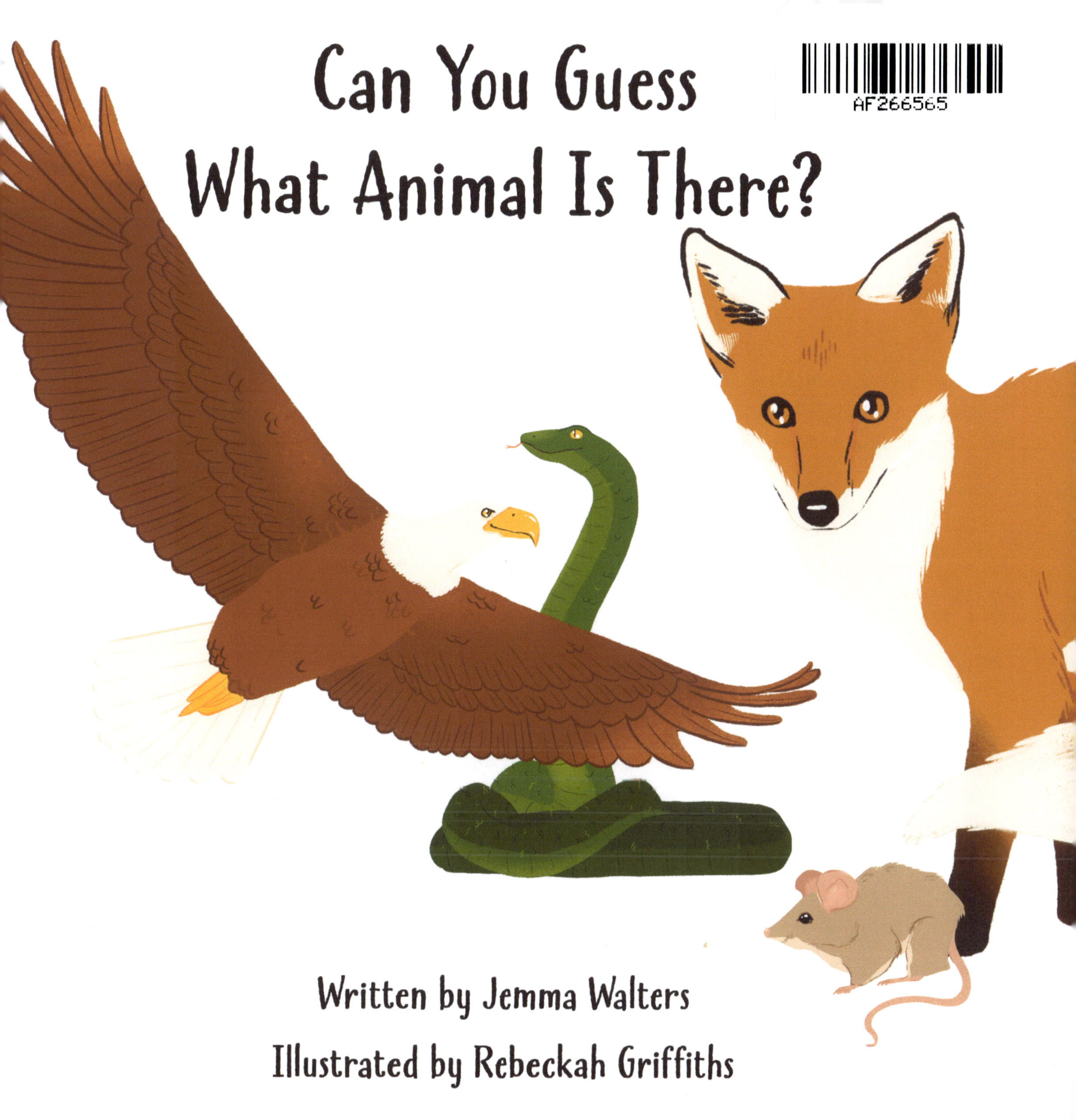

Can You Guess What Animal Is There?

Written by Jemma Walters

Illustrated by Rebeckah Griffiths

First published 2022
by Rowanvale Books Ltd,
The Gate,
Keppoch Street,
Roath,
Cardiff,
CF24 3JW

www.rowanvalebooks.com
Library Cataloguing in Publication Data.
A catalogue record for this book is available from the British Library.

ISBN: 978-1-913662-81-3

Scratching and scurrying

in the night with care.

Can you
guess what animal
is there?

It has tiny feet and makes a squeak;
it's much smaller than anyone you'll meet.

It has a long pink tail and a little pink nose,
beady eyes and tiny toes.

It loves to eat cheese and always
wants to explore, on little adventures to
see what's in store.

Can you

guess what animal

is there?

A mouse!

It has a big *bushy* tail and lives in a lair.

Can you
guess what animal
is there?

It loves to explore towns, cities and more.

It has whiskers and fur and has four paws.

Its fur comes in all shades of red, white and grey,

and it creeps very slyly to catch its prey.

Bish Bang Clitter Cling!

is the sound it makes searching through

crates and bins.

Looking for food to eat at night,

that tries to keep out of

the predator's sight.

Can you
guess what animal
is there?

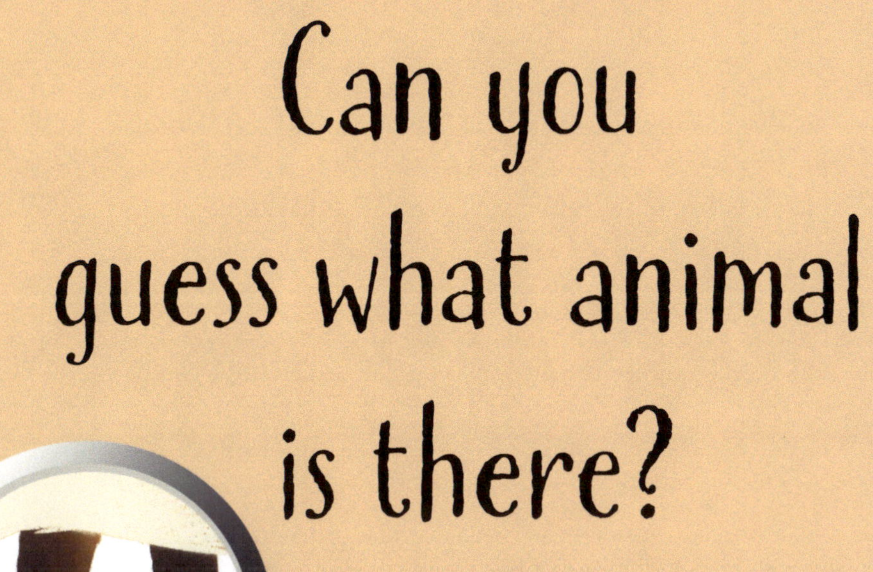

A fox!

It works in *flocks*, alone or in pairs.

Can you
guess what animal
is there?

It flies high in the sky and hovers
above the ground, searches for food and
swoops rapidly down.

It has feathers, two wings and a hooked beak; it
hunts its prey in a game of hide and seek.

It builds nests in tall trees
and is powerful and strong.
Very patient and still, waiting for its prey
to come along.

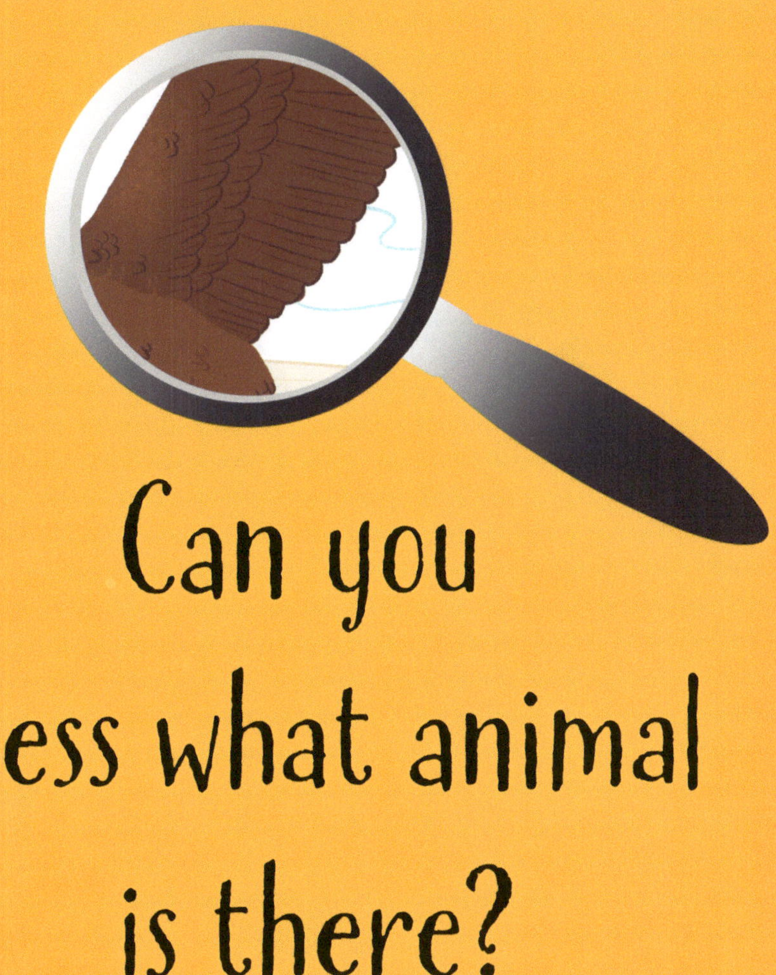

Can you
guess what animal
is there?

An eagle!

It *slithers* and *slides* and does not have any hair.

Can you
guess what animal
is there?

It's a cold-blooded reptile that varies in size.

There are many different species and they're

all hard to find.

It comes in many different colours such as
brown, green and white.

Some are patterned and some are bright.

It sheds its skin a few times a year.

A master of camouflage, it has nothing to fear.

Can you
guess what animal
is there?

A snake!

What Did You Think of Can You Guess What Animal is There?

A big thank you for purchasing this book. It means a lot that you chose this book specifically from such a wide range on offer. I do hope you enjoyed it.

Book reviews are incredibly important for an author. All feedback helps them improve their writing for future projects and for developing this edition. If you are able to spare a few minutes to post a review on Amazon, that would be much appreciated.

Publisher Information

Rowanvale Books provides publishing services to independent authors, writers and poets all over the globe. We deliver a personal, honest and efficient service that allows authors to see their work published, while remaining in control of the process and retaining their creativity. By making publishing services available to authors in a cost-effective and ethical way, we at Rowanvale Books hope to ensure that the local, national and international community benefits from a steady stream of good quality literature.

For more information about us, our authors or our publications, please get in touch.

www.rowanvalebooks.com
info@rowanvalebooks.com